D1389664

CAVALIER
KING CHARLES
SPANIELS

More and more people are appreciating
the charm and appeal of this attractive
breed whose history can be traced back
so far. And indeed, a Cavalier King
Charles is a delightful companion, who
repays his owner's care and attention
with an endearing devotion. Mrs. Stenning is a leading breeder and judge of
the breed, and her book contains all the
owner or potential owner of a Cavalier
King Charles should know, from
choosing a puppy to breeding and the
treatment of ailments.

LANDSCAPE WITH A HORSEMAN. Painted by A. Cuyp (mid 17th century) on exhibition at the Mauritshuis, The Hague, and reproduced by permission of the directors. It shows the similarity of the present day cavaliers with the toy spaniels to be found on the continent at that time.

Cavalier King Charles Spaniels

EILIDH M. STENNING

FOYLES HANDBOOKS
LONDON

ISBN 0 7071 0571 4

First published 1964
Reprinted 1973
Revised edition 1975
Reprinted 1978
Reprinted 1979
Reprinted 1980
Reprinted 1982

Published in Great Britain by
W. & G. Foyle Ltd.,
125 Charing Cross Road,
London, WC2H 0EB

Acknowledgements

I should like to express my thanks to those breeders who have been kind enough to allow me to use photographs of their dogs in this little book.

EILIDH M. STENNING

Printed and bound in Great Britain
at The Pitman Press, Bath

Contents

List of Illustrations

CHAPTER I

History of the Breed

✄

IT IS DIFFICULT to be sure of the exact origins of the King Charles Spaniel. It is certain that the dogs we now call Cavalier King Charles Spaniels are the direct descendants of the toy spaniels of the 16th, 17th, and 18th centuries. These dogs were to be seen in Italy, France, and Holland during that period, but there are considerable differences of opinion as to which of these countries could claim to have produced the first specimens. Evidence that there were small spaniels, which show great similarity to our present day Cavaliers, in these countries can be found in many of the paintings of the Old Masters. These can be seen, not only on the Continent, but in our own picture galleries and stately homes. The similarity is very well shown in the painting by Albert Cuyp, 'Landscape with horseman representing a member of the de Roovere family', which is reproduced in this volume by permission of the Directors of the MAURITSHUIS at the Hague, where the original can be seen.

The favourites of Royalty and the noble families of Europe for generations, these little spaniels were brought to England to become favourites at the Court of King Charles II. Hence the name King Charles Spaniel, for it was recorded that the Monarch was frequently accompanied by these little dogs. It is also probable that there were some of the toy spaniels in England earlier than that period. They enjoyed great popularity until they were ousted by Pugs. Later, when people began to take more interest in breeding pedigree dogs, and even started holding dog shows, it became fashionable to breed short-nosed dogs. The little spaniels' faces gradually got shorter and shorter until they became like The King Charles Spaniel as we know it today. These short-nosed spaniels became so popular that the old type, with the long nose, fine-pointed muzzle, and flat topped skull soon disappeared, and practically none of them were to be seen for about 100 years. It was not until 1926 that any move was made to breed back to the original type. In that year an American Citizen, Mr. Roswell Eldridge, visited this country. He was so concerned to find that the old type of King Charles Spaniel had been replaced by the flat-nosed variety that, in order to revive interest in the original type, he offered prizes of £25 at Cruft's Dog Show for 'The best Dog and best Bitch exhibited in a class for Blenheim Spaniels of the old type, as shown in the pictures of Charles II's time: long face, no stop, flat skull, not inclined to be "domed" – with spot on centre of skull'. These £25 prizes were offered each year for five years. In the first year only two entries were made but later, interest in reviving the old type of toy spaniel did begin to grow. A small group of breeders got together, with a view to forming a club and reviving the true old type King Charles Spaniel. They spent much time studying the dogs portrayed in the old pictures and in drawing up a standard of points to guide them in their breeding operations.

At that time of course, there were very few long-nosed dogs available, so progress was slow and very difficult. Breeders had to use 'Throw-outs' from the kennels of the breeders of the flat-faced variety – who were most co-operative and helpful. These early breeders have been accused of using other suitable breeds to get back the long noses, but this accusation is not justified, nor were the members of this small body in favour of breeding back in that way. They felt strongly that the only good way to breed back to the long noses was to do it through the long nosed 'Throw-outs', but it was a hard struggle. When they bred a litter, the puppies which were not considered good enough for the breeding programme were difficult to give away, let alone sell, although I believe there were one or two fortunate occasions when some were sold for as much as £2! When this happened it was looked upon as a rare piece of good fortune!

The present dog breeders certainly owe a big debt of gratitude for the keenness of those few pioneers.

In 1928 The Cavalier King Charles Spaniel Club was registered, with Mrs. Pitt as its first secretary.

The word 'Cavalier' was added to the name of the breed to distinguish it from the flat-nosed variety. It was felt that both types should have 'King Charles Spaniel' in their title, for they both spring from the same original stock.

Separate registration was granted by the Kennel Club in 1945, and in 1946 the first set of challenge certificates was offered. Since that time the breed has progressed, both in popularity and in numbers. Today we have over 1,500 registrations a year. There are many shows with classes for the breed, and these are usually well-filled, with plenty of admirers round the ringside to watch the judging. History has repeated itself with the cavalier once more the favoured pet of Royalty. Her Royal Highness Princess Margaret, Countess of Snowdon, has frequently been seen leading her cavalier 'Rowley'.

1973 has become a most important year for the history of this Royal breed with Messrs. Hall and Evans' young home-bred Blenheim dog 'Alansmere Aquarius' reaching every breeder's idea of the summit of achievement. At the age of 17 months this great little dog was not only Best of his breed at Cruft's 1973, but was judged Best Toy dog in the show by a second judge, and finally achieved the Supreme honour of being judged the Best Dog in the Show by yet a third judge. This was not only the first time a cavalier had attained this great honour but it was the first time it had ever been awarded to a Toy breed in the history of Cruft's Show. It was certainly an unmistakably Royal dog that showed his paces in the ring on that memorable evening. Apart from the honour he brought to his breed he brought especial honour to the breeders in the West of England – having been born and bred in his owner's kennels at Bristol – so his great win will live long in the memories of west country breeders especially. When he won at Cruft's he had achieved his second challenge Certificate that day and in fact had to wait nearly a month after Cruft's before he won his third challenge certificate at the Cavalier Club's Championship show – at the first opportunity he had of achieving the title of Champion Alansmere Aquarius – which he now carries with great honour.

1. CHAMPION ALANSMERE AQUARIUS. The first toy dog ever to be Crufts Supreme Champion (1973). Blenheim dog. Born 10.9.71. Bred and owned by Alan Hall and John Evans. *Sire:* Ch. Vairire Osiris. *Dam:* Ch. Alansmere McGoogans Maggle May

2. ANN'S SON. Blenheim dog. Born 29.4.27. Owner and breeder Miss
K. Mostyn Walker. *Sire:* Lord Pindi. *Dam:* Ann

3. CH. DAYWELL ROGER
Blenheim dog. Born 14.10.45.
Owned by Miss Jane Pitt
(now Mrs. Bowdler) and bred
by Mrs. Brierley. *Sire:*
Canonhill Richey. *Dam:*
Daywell Nell

Photo: H. J. Goater

4. **CH. DICKON OF LITTLEBREACH.** Blenheim dog. Born 1.12.61. Owned and bred by Mrs. Percival. *Sire:* Hillbarn Fabian. *Dam:* Ch. Amanda of Littlebreach.

Photo: Thos Fall

5. **CH. PARGETER BOB UP.** Blenheim dog. Born 7.1.58. Owned and bred by Mrs. Keswick. *Sire:* Ch. Abelard of Ttiweh. *Dam:* Ch. Pargeter Phyllida

Photo: C. M. Cooke

CHAPTER II

The Breed Standard

BEFORE a novice can read a Breed Standard with any real understanding it is necessary to have at least an elementary knowledge of the anatomy of the dog. If you are intending to breed and show, and perhaps later to judge, it is vitally important that you know the anatomy and also the various terms in use in referring to the structure of the dog. A study of illustrations is the easiest way to acquire this knowledge in the first place – but needs to be followed by handling a dog and feeling him all over for yourself as well as studying his movement.

As there are two different varieties of King Charles Spaniel it might be as well to note here the chief difference between them – and that is the head. In the King Charles Spaniel (or 'Charlie' as he is sometimes called) the head is domed and the ears set rather low. The nose is very short and up-turned to meet the skull with a deep stop. In the Cavalier King Charles Spaniel the skull is not domed at all, the ears are set fairly high, the muzzle is long, with a very shallow stop, gently tapering to the tip of the nose. The other main difference between the two breeds is in the size. The King Charles Standard weight is from 6 lbs. – 12 lbs. whereas the Cavalier King Charles Standard weight is 10 lbs. – 18 lbs. so that he is, or should be, noticeably larger than the flat-faced variety.

THE CAVALIER KING CHARLES SPANIEL

Standard of points for the breed

HEAD AND SKULL – Head almost flat between the ears, without dome. Stop shallow; length from base of stop to tip about 1½ inches. Nostrils should be well developed and the pigment black. Muzzle well tapered to the point. Lips well covering, but not hound-like.

EYES – Large, dark and round, but not prominent. The eyes should be spaced well apart.

EARS – Long and set high, with plenty of feather.

MOUTH – Level.

NECK – Should be well set on.

FOREQUARTERS – Shoulders not too straight. Legs; moderate bone, straight.

BODY – Should be short-coupled, with plenty of spring of rib. Back level. Chest moderate, leaving ample heart room.

HINDQUARTERS – Legs; moderate bone, straight.

FEET – Compact, well-cushioned, and well feathered.

TAIL – The docking of tails is optional. The length of the tail should be in balance with the body.

COAT – Long, silky, and free from curl. A slight wave is permissible. There should be plenty of feather.

COLOUR –

Black and Tan: Raven black with tan markings above eyes, on cheeks, inside ears, on chest, legs, and underside of tail. Tan should be bright.

Ruby: Whole-coloured rich red.

Blenheim: Rich chestnut markings well broken-up on a pearly white ground. The markings should be evenly divided on the head, leaving room between the ears for the much valued lozenge mark or spot, a unique characteristic of this breed.

RIGHT • THE CAVALIER HEAD • WRONG

FLAT SCULL

DOMED SCULL

EARS SET HIGH

EARS SET LOW

SHALLOW STOP

DEEP STOP & SHORT MUZZLE

MUZZLE TAPERED BUT NOT PINCHED

PINCHED MUZZLE

GOOD LIPS

HOUND LIPS

LEVEL MOUTH

SCISSOR-BITE TEETH

MOUTH UNDERSHOT

MOUTH OVERSHOT

Fig. 1.

Tricolour: Black and white, well spaced and broken-up, with tan markings over the eyes, on cheeks, inside ears, inside legs and on underside of tail.

Any other colour is most undesirable.

WEIGHT AND SIZE – Weight 10 lbs. to 18 lbs. A small well-balanced dog well between these weights is desirable.

NOTE – *Docking* is optional and is usually done at about five days old, and about one third of the tail is generally removed.

Dew Claws should be removed. This can be done from three days old, or at the same time as docking.

For the benefit of the novice perhaps a little elaboration on some of the points may be useful, particularly if studied with the head and body diagrams. For instance it is difficult to make clear the difference between the 'tapered' muzzle and the 'pinched' muzzle. This latter is exaggerated in the drawing in order to give the pinched look but, on the actual dog, this faulty muzzle can be spotted easily when compared with the good-headed dog, because the face not only looks rather mean and pinched but it can be seen that the contour of the face falls away below the eyes. In the dog with a well-tapered muzzle there is plenty of filling below the eyes and it is this which makes all the difference. It is difficult to show this in a sketch.

Mouth. The novice may feel he wants to know a little more about this than is given in the Standard, particularly as to teeth. In a perfect mouth the adult dog should have forty-two teeth. *The Upper Jaw* has twelve molars (or side teeth) two canines (the rather large pointed teeth at each side of the mouth and immediately in front of the molars – they look like fangs) and six incisors (the small flat teeth across the front of the jaw). *The Lower Jaw* has fourteen molars, two canines and six incisors.

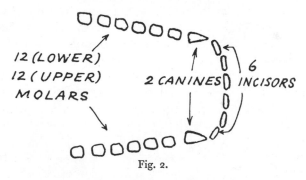

Fig. 2.

To have a perfect mouth a dog must not only have a full set of teeth placed correctly and evenly, but his 'bite' must be correct, i.e. the way the teeth meet. Cavaliers should have a level mouth with the top teeth just closing over the bottom teeth in front – a 'scissor bite' – because the lower edges of the top incisors over-lap the top of the bottom incisors very slightly, in the way that one blade of a pair of scissors very slightly overlaps the other. The teeth should be set evenly in the jaw in the form of a U, slightly flattened at the curved end, which of course is the front of the mouth. The pattern is the same top and bottom.

Faulty or Bad Mouths. In these we may find undershot or overshot jaws – causing faulty 'bites', faulty dentition (i.e. not the correct number of teeth or teeth not in the correct formation). The incisors may be in a ragged or uneven line, and sometimes we find the canines tending to point out sideways a bit instead of being in an even line with the molars.

Neck. A Cavalier should have a nice reach of neck and the neckline from the occiput should continue in a graceful line along the back. A short thick neck is a fault and makes the dog look very unbalanced.

Forequarters. The shoulder blade should be well laid back (see Fig. 4). If it is too upright you get the forelegs

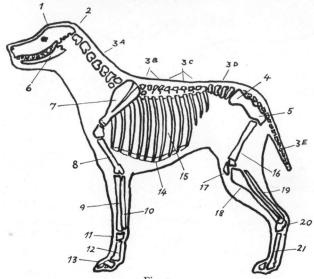

Fig. 3.

1. Skull	6. Jaw bone	14. Breast bone
2. Occiput	7. Shoulder blade	(Sternum)
3. Vertebrae:	(Scapula)	15. Ribs
A. 7 Cervical	8. Humerus	16. Femur
B. 4 Dorsal	9. Radius	17. Patella
C. 5 Lumbar	10. Ulna	18. Tibia
D. 6 Sacral	11. Carpus	19. Fibula
E. Tail Vertebrae	12. Metacarpals	20. Hock (Tarsus)
4. Ilium	13. Phalanges (toe	21. Metarsus
5. Pelvis	bones)	

out at elbow, giving bad movement. An upright shoulder usually gives a short neck-line and a long back-line.

Hindquarters. These should be straight viewed from behind. Viewed from the side there should be good angulation at the knee (or stifle) joint so that the tibia and neckline would be on the same diagonal line drawn from occiput to hock joint. The hocks should be straight (see diagram).

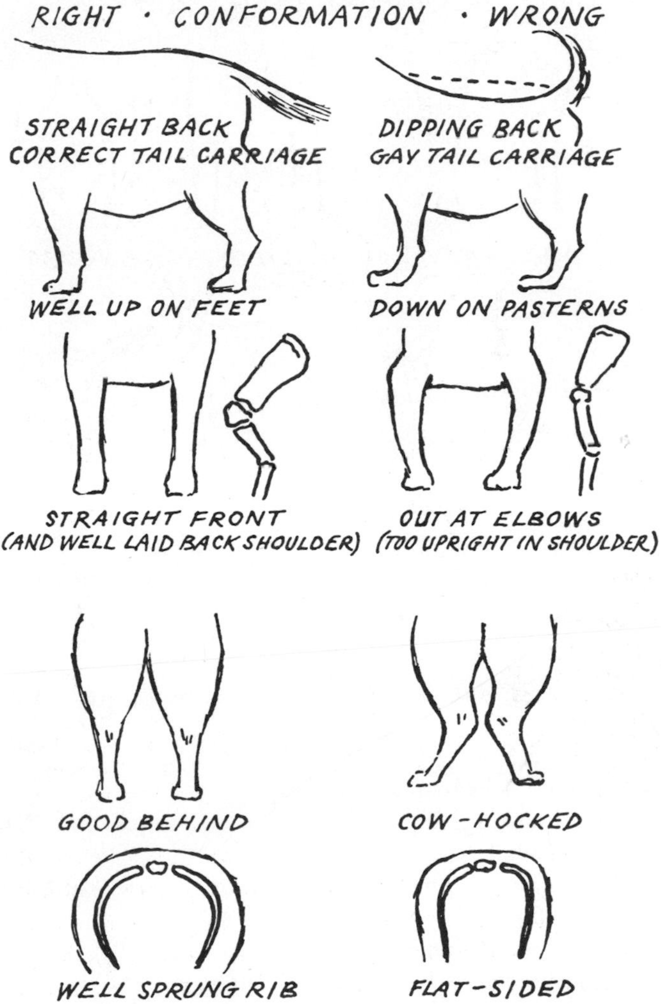

RIGHT · CONFORMATION · WRONG

STRAIGHT BACK
CORRECT TAIL CARRIAGE

DIPPING BACK
GAY TAIL CARRIAGE

WELL UP ON FEET

DOWN ON PASTERNS

STRAIGHT FRONT
(AND WELL LAID BACK SHOULDER)

OUT AT ELBOWS
(TOO UPRIGHT IN SHOULDER)

GOOD BEHIND

COW-HOCKED

WELL SPRUNG RIB

FLAT-SIDED

Fig. 4.

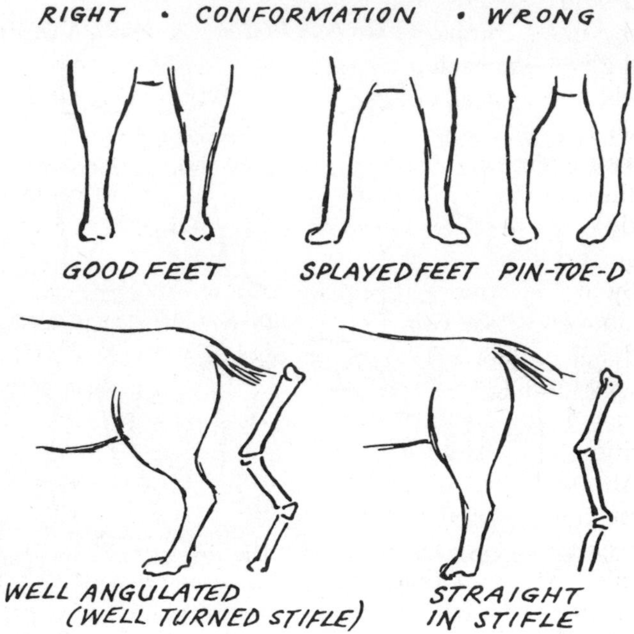

RIGHT • CONFORMATION • WRONG

GOOD FEET   SPLAYED FEET   PIN-TOE-D

WELL ANGULATED   STRAIGHT
(WELL TURNED STIFLE)   IN STIFLE

Fig. 5.

Faults. Bad mouth (overshot, undershot, wry mouth etc.).

Light Eyes.

Off-colour – brown or putty nose.

White markings on whole-colours (Rubies and Black and Tans).

Very heavily marked particolours (Tricolours and Blenheims).

Coarseness of type.

Unsoundness.

Bad Temperament (nervous or bad tempered).

Characteristics. Cavaliers are attractive, friendly, and essentially gay little dogs. They are very companionable and enjoy human company to the full. They also enjoy each other's company. If you have half a dozen Cavaliers and give them each a separate basket you will almost certainly find that all six are piled into one basket while the other five are left empty. It is rarely that you will find a Cavalier sleeping alone if there are other dogs or cats in the house. He will invariably seek out one of them and settle down to sleep up against it, whether it is a cat or dog.

By nature these dogs are very adaptable, and very anxious to please you, so you will find them easy to train and naturally inclined to be obedient. Proof of this is the great measure of success met with by owners who have trained their Cavaliers to work in obedience competitions, competing with all other breeds.

Although the Cavalier is classified as a toy dog, one must emphasize that they are not 'lap-dogs'. They are toy spaniels, and they have the sporting instincts of the spaniel. Many of them have proved their worth in the field and out with the guns. They are not gun shy as a rule, have good mouths, and can retrieve small game. Obviously they could not bring in anything very large, but they think nothing of carrying home a rabbit nearly as large as themselves. The hunting instinct is very much with them and, if you live in the country you will need to watch them, especially if there are several, when you go for a walk. As a rule they are very good about following, but they are very likely to get the urge to hunt and you may see them disappear into the woods giving tongue in true spaniel fashion. They will, in this event, probably be deaf to all your urgent whistles or calling to heel. They will return later, probably very muddy, and maybe with a peace offering in the form of a rabbit to drop at your feet, but almost certainly quite unrepentant. They have enjoyed themselves far too much for that!

Lastly I think it would be as well to mention that they usually love water and will plunge in, if they find any, quite regardless of whether it is clean or rather stagnant and smelly. It's all the same to them.

CHAPTER III

Choosing Your Dog

I F YOU are looking for a pet cavalier you will not need to concern yourself with show points or details of pedigrees as you would if you were looking for a show and breeding dog. You will be mainly concerned with a dog that is attractive to look at and has a nice character and personality. Your first consideration will probably be that of sex. If you have made your decision on this point, all is well and you can go ahead to the next but, if you are uncertain about the sex you want, the following notes may prove useful.

BITCHES. Some people consider that a bitch makes a better pet than a dog because they think them more gentle and affectionate. This of course is a matter of opinion and open to argument, as are all opinions. There are others who say they would never keep a bitch because she must be 'shut up' for three weeks every six months or so, and some who say that it is unfair and inadvisable for the health of a bitch not to let her breed one litter. I am not very keen on selling bitches to people who have no intention of letting them have just one litter, especially cavalier bitches, because they are, as a rule, excellent and devoted mothers and enjoy their maternity. As far as the other objection goes – it does of course have its disadvantages and is at best a little nuisance, but there are excellent products on the market now which, although not dispensing with the need for keeping the bitch very carefully confined at these times, can greatly minimise the attraction for male dogs, and it is possible, with their aid, to exercise a bitch *on a lead* on public roads and commons during her heat without suffering too much nuisance from unwanted suitors.

DOGS. A number of people insist on having a dog for a pet, explaining that it is far less trouble. Others disagree, saying that dogs are more difficult to house-train than bitches, that they are apt to roam more, especially when neighbouring bitches are on heat, and also that they frequently develop unpleasant and embarrassing habits. Again these are opinions, and open to argument. So, the question of the sex of your pet is one that only you can decide, having heard the various arguments for and against in each case. When you have made your decision, do not allow yourself to be talked out of it: you are the most likely person to know what will suit you best.

It is perhaps interesting to note here that, until comparatively recently, purchasers requiring pets invariably stipulated that they must have a dog, whereas of recent years there has been a marked swing in favour of bitches.

COLOUR is possibly the next consideration – entirely a matter of personal opinion and one that you can decide upon after visiting a show or private kennels and looking at the four different colours available in the breed.

AGE. This is an important consideration. There are some cases, usually where an elderly, or possibly invalid person, wants a new pet, in which an adult trained dog is considered the best but, other things being equal, I would recommend the choice of a puppy of about eight – twelve weeks. It does require the devoted time and attention of its new owner for the first few weeks but, if this is freely given, there is no doubt that it pays dividends.

There are of course other more general things to be considered such as where you will get your puppy, how much you can afford to pay for him, and the extremely important one of how you will choose him and what to look for in making the choice.

As far as where to get the puppy is concerned – if you know of a reliable breeder, your path is easy, as it also is if you have a friend who already has a satisfactory puppy and can give you the address of the kennels from which it came. If you have no such sources, you can visit a show where you know there will be classes for the breed and talk to exhibitors, making enquiries as to whether any of them have puppies available, and getting addresses so that you may pay a visit to their kennels. Information about shows can be got from the weekly dog papers (Dog World and Our Dogs) which appear every Friday. Addresses of breeders can be obtained from these papers, and also from The Kennel Club, 1–4 Clarges Street, Piccadilly, W1Y 8AB. Make appointments to visit any kennels you think suitable and see the owners and the dogs in their home surroundings. Look for clean kennels and clean, healthy, gay, and active dogs that are friendly and good-tempered and not cowed or nervous. When choosing a puppy from a litter look for a plump, compact, sturdy puppy that is active and happy. Don't choose one that cringes or runs to the far corner of the kennel or pen. The puppy with character and personality is the one who is curious to know who and what you are and is bold enough to come and find out.

If you go to a breeder for your puppy you will be buying it from someone who knows all about its breeding and who, in most cases has probably had it in their care since birth, although there are of course exceptions to this where a breeder has loaned a bitch to someone on breeding terms and takes the puppy or puppies when they are weaned, or similar instances. If you go to a pet shop to buy a puppy it is a different matter, and you will need to remember that you will then have to pay to the shop enough to cover what the shopkeeper has paid to the breeder for the puppy plus something extra to cover his overheads and allow a reasonable margin of profit. In the case of cavaliers it is unlikely that you would find one for sale in a pet shop. Should you enquire for one the owner would get you one from a breeder if possible, adding something to the price on the way, as is only reasonable.

Having chosen your puppy it is a wise precaution to ask to be allowed to arrange for a veterinary surgeon to examine it before completing the purchase. No wise breeder would refuse this request for, apart from anything else, it takes responsibility off their shoulders as to the good health of the puppy at the time they sell it to you.

Choosing a Dog for Show and Breeding

This is a very different matter from choosing a 'pet', and there is no question as to the wisdom of learning as much as you can about the breed before you set out to buy your show puppy. Study the breed standard, go to the shows and watch the dogs and the judging, talk to the exhibitors and experienced breeders, note the pedigrees of the dogs, and generally pick up every available scrap of information that you can. Above all, after watching as many judges at work as you can, try and get your eye in so that you have an idea of the type of dog you want and feel that you will recognise the type when you see it. Your foundation stock is so important that it is worthwhile doing all you can to ensure that you start with the right material.

When you feel you are ready to embark on the purchase of the founder or founders of your kennel, make up your mind not to be in too much hurry, but to look at what you are offered with a critical eye and, if it doesn't seem just what you want, wait a bit and see whether you find something better. When buying foundation stock for a kennel the old adage can well be adapted to 'Buy in haste, repent at leisure'.

I would not advise starting with a dog and bitch, but rather with either one or two good brood bitches. From these, mated wisely to suitable well-known sires, you could have the chance of breeding yourself a good enough dog to keep for stud at a later date. This also has the advantage of giving a beginner time to gain a little more experience before embarking on the added responsibilities and complications of a stud dog and his management.

A brood bitch should come from strong, healthy stock, and be of the best breeding available. She should be of a really good all-round type, with no really bad faults. Look for a well-made, sound bitch, with a good spring of rib, dark eyes and nose pigment, good body colouring and a good mouth and, above all, a good temperament. A shy, nervous bitch is not a good brood bitch.

In choosing a show puppy, if you have an eye for a dog, you can judge your puppy reasonably well at two or three months, but obviously there are many chances you must take in buying at that age. With a cavalier I think that the most unpredictable thing about a young puppy is the mouth which, in this breed, it is not possible to be absolutely sure of until the second teeth are through, and even then in some cases I have seen a slightly doubtful mouth right itself after a year old. It is certainly true to say that a puppy of say nine or ten weeks with a perfect looking mouth can end up undershot, and vice versa.

Do not think that because a dog has a good pedigree it is necessarily a good show dog. Remember that a litter may contain a champion and other winners and a puppy that has too many faults to make a show dog, but *they all have the same pedigree*.

Picking a Puppy from the Nest

I find the best time to do this is when the puppies are about one – two hours old but, apart from one's own litters, this is obviously not a practical way. With my own litters I always pick the puppies then. First I look for the neatest squarest, and most generally compact looking puppy, one with well sprung ribs and a balanced look about it. I look at the head and choose one with a big bump of loose skin over the nose and of course pay some attention to colour markings. Although during the course of their growth in the following two or three months I usually find that I change my mind several times as to the best puppy, it is quite surprising how often the one I first picked, about an hour after they were born, is the one I go back to in the end, finding it has after all turned out to be the best. It is however a very difficult if not impossible thing to try and teach anyone else how to pick a puppy. There is always a 'something' about your best puppy that strikes you, but that is difficult to explain to someone else. In other words each person must develop their 'eye for a dog' themselves and be able to interpret what they see. If you are trying to pick a puppy from a litter at about eight weeks old, you want to look for a well-balanced compact and sturdy puppy. I think this question of a well-balanced look is important for, if the puppy has this look, it probably is a well-proportioned, well-made dog. Don't go for one that looks very long in the back or 'straggly', or very flat-sided, and don't choose one with a 'pinched' look about it's head and face. Look for a well-proportioned head with a shallow stop and rather down pointing muzzle, that has a nice bump over the nose. You also want to look for long ear leathers and a good width between the eyes. Look for good eye and nose pigment. Very blue looking eyes at eight weeks or more usually mean light eyes when adult. If you are choosing a Blenheim puppy you

6. A typical litter of 8 week old puppies

7. A promising trio of 3 month old puppies

Photo: F. W. Simms

8. CH. CHERRYCOURT WAKE ROBIN. Blenheim dog. Born 3.9.64. Owned and bred by Mrs. Stenning. *Sire:* Ch. Pargeter Trillium of Ttiweh. *Dam:* Pargeter Souvenir

Photo: Sally Anne Thompson.

9. CH. AMELIA OF LAGUNA. Blenheim bitch. Born 22.2.59. Owned by Mrs. Cryer and bred by Miss L. Mackay. *Sire:* Ch. Aloysius of Sunninghill. *Dam:* Pargeter Paprika

Photo: Sally Anne Thompson

must remember they are born almost lemon and white and so, because they may look very pale to you when they are in the nest, it doesn't mean they will be as pale when they are older. You can really get a better idea of their future colour by the depth of colour on the ear leathers. This also applies to ruby puppies. Big knobbly joints and feet usually mean big dogs so, if you don't want a big one choose one with small neat feet and joints.

CHAPTER IV

Early Training

WHEN YOU have chosen your puppy find out exactly how he has been fed and, when you take him home, change his diet as little as possible. You should also find out if, and when, he was wormed. Most people worm puppies at six weeks. If this has not been done it is something that you will have to attend to after the puppy has settled down with you. If he has been wormed at six weeks you need not do any more until he is three months, when it is advisable to check again and dose if need be. Always get worm pills for small puppies from a veterinary surgeon, who will prescribe something suitable. This is much better than buying pills in a packet from a shop, although the well-known makes of worm pills are perfectly all right for older dogs.

When you get home give your puppy his bed in his own corner out of a draught – a wooden box from the grocer that has a piece cut out of one side so that he can get in and out easily, will do very well to start with, and it is better to save the more expensive box or basket that you may have in mind for him until he is over the teething and chewing stage. An old piece of rug or blanket in the box will complete his bed, and is easily washed out and kept clean. Remember he will take a little time to adjust himself to his new surroundings and may also miss the company of his brothers and sisters. Let him do this adjusting quietly and don't let every one keep picking him up and fussing him all the time. Puppies are like babies and need plenty of sleep and quiet during their early development. Teach him to settle down in his bed for part of each day and not to mind being left on his own at times. This will save you endless trouble in the future. The dog that cannot be left alone because he howls and barks is utterly miserable himself and also makes his owner's life a misery and worry. In fact he will probably end up by having to be got rid of because the neighbours complain about the noise every time he is left alone in the house.

The importance of early training cannot be stressed too much. Cavaliers are very adaptable, very anxious to please their owners, and so not difficult to train. Therefore do give up that little extra time to give him the early training he needs to make your life and his as happy as they can be. The dividend reaped will make the training time spent in the early days well worth while.

HOUSE-TRAINING is a matter of perseverence and patience. Put him out very frequently at first, gradually lengthening the periods between the outings. If he is praised every time he does as he should and is brought in at once, he will soon learn the purpose of the outing.

TRAINING TO COLLAR AND LEAD. This is best done by putting a soft collar or a very light leather one round his neck just before feeding him. As soon as he has had his meal the first time take the collar off. Leave it on a little longer each time until he is quite happy with it. As soon as he is completely at home in a collar put a light lead on and take him out, but don't let him feel any pull on the lead. Put him on the ground with the lead slack and call him to you, let him come along with you as you talk to him and encourage him, keeping the lead slack all the time until he gets well used to it. Do this for a few minutes only each day to start with, and you will soon find that he gets quite used to it. Never drag a puppy on a lead, and never allow him to pull you along. A well-trained dog should always walk beside his owner on a slack lead. Be careful not to walk a young growing puppy too far.

CAR TRAINING. This must be started as young as possible, and I strongly advise starting by 'boxing' the puppy in the car. It is extremely useful to be able to put your dog in a box or basket for travelling, and so you should get him used to this in the early days. Later you can easily teach him where you want him to travel in your car and he will soon learn 'his' place. You will then have a dog that will travel either free in the car or in a box or basket, whichever happens to be convenient. If you start by letting him be free in the car, he will of course be more difficult to train to a box afterwards. If you do start your puppy getting used to car travel *early* I don't think you will find he is bothered by car sickness. He may be a little sick for the first ride or two but will soon get over that. Training him to travel in a box or basket first is a help in this respect, for he will get used to the motion of the car while he is in a fairly confined space. I think most dogs are car sick because they won't settle down quietly but try and travel standing up and often looking out of windows. Seeing things moving past the windows makes the dog feel excited and perhaps he gets a sort of nervous tension which produces the sickness. My reasons for saying this are because I have had one or two dogs who were invariably sick if they travelled 100 miles or so to a show free in the car. They were dogs that had not been used to a car from babyhood, and they never seemed to settle down and sleep on the outward journey in the morning. They would sit up, or stand up, and be looking out of the window. I am sure that this, combined with the excitement of going to a show, caused them to be sick. These same dogs were *never* sick during the 100 miles return journey. They were usually a bit

10. CH. STELLERS EIDER OF PANTISA. Ruby dog. Born 31.8.68.
Owned by Mr. & Mrs. Gillies and bred by Mrs. Halsall. *Sire:* Ttiweh Black
Prince O'Cockpen. *Dam:* Cuckoo of Pantisa

Photo: C. M. Cooke

11. CHERRYCOURT SPRING TIDE. Tricolour dog. Born 4.7.68.
Owned and bred by Mrs. Stenning. *Sire:* Ch. Cherrycourt Wake Robin.
Dam: Cherrycourt April Morn

Photo: Thos. Fall

12. CH. ALOYSIUS OF SUNNINGHILL. Tricolour dog. Born 27.11.55. Owned by Miss P. Turle and bred by Grant Wilson. *Sire:* Amulet of Sunninghill. *Dam:* Louisa of Sunninghill.

Photo: F. W. Simms

tired after a long day and would settle down on the back seat and sleep all the way home.

People have produced all sorts of remedies for car sickness in dogs. I have tried most of them at one time or another but so far have not found anything that worked consistently with even one dog, let alone with different dogs. A chain hung on the car and touching the ground is a favourite but, it *is* necessary for the chain to be in contact with the ground for it to be effective. These chains may well touch the ground when the car is stationary, but if you look at the chain fitted to any car travelling ahead of you it is never on the ground but always blowing out behind and above the ground. Another theory is that if the dog has access to green grass while travelling in the car it will prevent sickness. I have never found this makes any difference. Lastly there are all the sedative and seasick pills which are said to be effective. I am afraid my best advice for a dog that is known to travel badly is not to worry about trying every remedy under the sun. Just arm yourself with plenty of newspaper spread all over the seat etc., let the dog out for a minute or two if he looks like being sick, and clear up the mess with the newspaper if you are too late to get him out in time!

I take my dogs about in the car a tremendous amount and have never had trouble with the ones that have been trained to it from babyhood – except possibly on the first outing or two.

Lastly, when you leave your dog in the car, don't leave the car in the hot sun – do see that a window is open enough to give the dog air but not enough for him to climb out – and do *not* tie the dog up, or leave him with a trailing lead attached to his collar. This can get caught up in something and be dangerous. If you are leaving him for any length of time leave a dish of water for him. Do not forget to empty it before you drive off!

CHAPTER V

General Care

✕

A HEALTHY dog needs fresh air, exercise, and grooming, as well as good food and fresh water for drinking.

Grooming

This should be done every day and will take about five minutes. A good comb through to see there are no tangles or knots, especially round the ears and under them and between the legs and the under body, followed by a brushing along the lie of the coat, should suffice to keep the coat clean and free of tangles or felted up fur. A quick examination of the eyes and insides of the ears will show whether any cleaning is necessary. A Mason Pearson type or nylon brush is suitable and the comb should be a metal one. I find Spratts No. 92 the most useful size, although for a very heavily coated dog you may find a coarser grade better. If you live in the country near farm animals, and poultry, rabbits, game birds, squirrels, hedgehogs, etc. you will need to watch carefully for fleas, lice, and ticks as dogs, however clean they are kept, can easily pick these up during field walks. A No. 93 nit comb with a handle is best for removing fleas from the coat. A dusting over with Derris dust occasionally is a great deterrent to fleas and lice. DO NOT USE POWDER CONTAINING D.D.T. as this is dangerous for dogs. Derris powder can be bought in puffer cartons from Boots for about 12–15p.

If you do find the dog has *lice* you can soon get rid of them by bathing with Selsun *but this must be used with the utmost care, especially seeing that you do not get any near the dog's eyes, and following the instructions carefully.*

Fleas can be got rid of by bathing in Kurmange. *Ticks* must be removed by putting a drop of liquid paraffin or olive oil on the head of the tick, this loosens the grip in the dog's skin and the tick can be removed with forceps. If you try and do it without the oil you may leave the head in the skin.

Apart from this, and the need for bathing before a show, I do not recommend bathing dogs often. With regular grooming it is not necessary, and if carried out too frequently it does take the natural oil out of the skin and dry it up.

Should you find your dog's skin a bit scurfy you can get rid of this by rubbing in some Vaseline hair tonic, but this is a very oily mixture and you will need to keep your dog off furniture while the hair tonic is in the coat. You can also use a Vosene shampoo for scurfy coats.

Toe nails. These will need to be kept trimmed in the same way as human nails need trimming regularly. A pair of dog nail clippers is the best thing to use and you must be careful not to cut off too near the quick or you will find the nails bleed. With light coloured nails you can easily see where it begins, but it is not easy to see with dark nails and you have to guess.

Inoculation. This should be done as soon as possible after eight weeks by your Veterinary Surgeon. It is advisable for the dog to have a 'Booster' injection at about one year old.

Housing

This really depends largely on the amount of space you have available and how many dogs you intend keeping. If you intend to go in for breeding in a big way you will of course need good dry, draught-proof outdoor kennels with wire runs attached. Cavaliers are very hardy and, provided the kennels are really dry and draught-proof and have good bedding, they can live out all the year round. In this case I would recommend putting them to sleep in pairs, or even using a larger kennel and letting several dogs share it, supplying them with a large sleeping box into which they can all get at once. As mentioned in an earlier chapter this breed much prefers sharing a bed to sleeping alone, and by sharing a bed they keep each other warm.

If you decide to have a small enough number to keep in the house, which I think is really the best way to keep Cavaliers, for they love human company, they will soon learn where their beds are and be quite happy to retire to them when you are busy, if you train them to do this on command. If you are keeping them in the house, and breeding, it is really rather necessary to have one room, preferably on the ground floor and with easy access to the exercising ground, set aside as a dog room. Ideally it should have water laid on and a good deep sink with a wooden draining board. This can be used for washing dogs and also for washing their blankets, brushes, and even food dishes. A wooden draining board is much better than any other kind for dogs to be put on while they are being dried. In this room you can keep all your dog paraphernalia, do your whelping and mating, and of course have pens in it for the small puppies and for nursing mothers. It should have at least one good cupboard and a firm table. A chest of drawers is very useful if you have room for it. A gas ring or small stove is of great benefit, but is not always easy to arrange. The floor should be covered with linoleum or other waterproof material that will wash over easily, and some form of heating *that is safely protected from the dogs* is needed. Oil stoves are not suitable.

Feeding

Most Cavaliers are greedy by nature and so not difficult to feed. Nevertheless they do need proper feeding. The staple diet should consist of meat, either raw or cooked, and biscuit meal. I recommend Terrier grade for adult Cavaliers, and prefer to soak it in stock or, failing that, a little water, half an hour before feeding, rather than feed it quite dry. Meat, whether raw or cooked, needs to be cut up into fairly small pieces or minced coarsely, before feeding. If given in large lumps the dogs swallow it whole and do not digest it properly and so do not get the full benefit from it. Dogs like a little variety in their food and the meat can be varied sometimes with well cooked tripe, or paunch, or fish. Any white fish, or fresh herrings are good, but of course no bones must be given. The best way is to boil the fish in water until all the bones are quite soft, then they can be chopped up with the fish and all put back into the stock they were boiled in and allowed to cool in a basin in the 'fridge, when it will be found that you have a good fish brawn all ready to mix with the biscuit. The same sort of treatment can be used for calves' heads and sheeps' heads, both of which make excellent dog meat. In this case you boil the heads in water until the meat falls easily off the bones. Put the heads on to a board and take the meat off the bones, making sure no small bones or chips are mixed in with the meat. Chop it all on the board into fairly small pieces. Strain the stock into a basin (this will make sure no bone chips are left in that) and then mix all the chopped up meat into it, cool it, and you will have a good meat brawn which will keep for about a week in a refrigerator. Other forms of meat which can be used include horse meat, heart, liver, melts etc. Some people feed lights but there is really very little nourishment to be derived from it.

Do not feed pork, salt or pickled meats, as these are not good for dogs.

If you have a kennel you will of course have to organise regular deliveries of meat either through one of the dog meat firms or a pet shop, or possibly your butcher will be able to supply you. *Biscuit* can best be bought in 1 cwt. sacks from the various biscuit firms, and it is of course much cheaper to do this than to buy it in small quantities. If you only have one or two pets to feed you will probably be able to arrange for small amounts of meat pieces to be supplied by your own butcher, and most grocers and corn chandlers sell small packets of dog biscuit as well as loose biscuit by the pound.

Bones. Only large bones should be given to dogs. NO chop or small rib bones, no mutton shoulder blade bones, and no poultry, game or fish bones. These all splinter and are not safe for a dog.

Feeding times. Different people have different ideas about the number of meals a dog needs and the best times to feed. I do not think either matters very much if the dogs are doing well and the feeding is regular. My own feeling is that one main meal in the morning fairly early and a snack meal after midday is quite a good idea. I am not very keen on feeding late in the day as I think it better for the dogs to have opportunity for exercise after meals. I do not like only one meal a day, given in the evening. If only one meal is to be given I feel it is better at midday or in the morning. If fed only at night, the dog sleeps on a full stomach and does all his energetic walks and exercise during the day on a more or less empty stomach.

It is important, when feeding dogs, to put their food down in clean dishes and to pick up the dish as soon as the dog has finished eating. NEVER leave food down all day. If the dog doesn't finish what you have given him, pick up the dish and take it away. If your dog gets used to a regular feeding time you should have no trouble. Once you start leaving dishes of food around all day, or coaxing and playing with the food to make a dog eat up, you are in for endless trouble and will soon have a faddy and difficult dog to feed. With a sick dog it may of course be necessary to do a little coaxing, but that is the only time it should be so. One does sometimes get an 'only' dog which is tricky to feed or won't eat his food, but it won't hurt him to go without for a day or two. Try putting his food down at regular times and, if he takes no interest pick it up at once. Probably after a few days he will feel hungry and decide not to miss the opportunity when the food is there.

Water. All dogs should have a bowl of fresh clean water always available for drinking.

CHAPTER VI

Some Common Ailments and Their Remedies

CAVALIERS are normally strong, healthy, active dogs and very hardy, and with proper housing, feeding, and care you should not have much trouble with their health. If you treat your dogs in the same way as a sensible mother treats her children you will not go far wrong.

ABSCESSES. These require a hot poultice to draw the matter from the abscess. Kaolin makes a good poultice. A little vaseline gently smeared over the place is helpful in preventing the poultice from sticking to the coat and skin. Be careful to test the poultice with the back of your hand before you apply it, so that you don't put it on the dog too hot.

ANAL GLAND. If you notice the dog rubbing itself along the ground in a sitting position it may mean worms, or it may mean that the anal gland is blocked. This gland is to be found under the tail and when blocked needs very gently squeezing between the finger and thumb in order to empty it. An experienced breeder or a Veterinary Surgeon will show you just how to do this, it is a very simple operation when you know how. Care is needed in carrying out the squeezing and it is a good thing to wear rubber gloves. If you have a scratch or sore place on your hand or finger then rubber gloves are very desirable for, should you get any of the liquid you have expressed from the gland on to a scratch, it might lead to trouble.

It is a good idea to squeeze this gland gently every three months or so to ensure it doesn't get blocked and form an abscess, which is extremely painful for the dog.

CHILLS are often caused because a dog comes in wet and cold and is not given a rub down, especially taking care to dry the legs and tummy. It is particularly necessary to do this with Cavaliers if they have been out in snow, for they love to plunge about in soft snow. If you think the dog has a chill give a warm milk drink, or milk, sugar or honey, and brandy and keep warm and on a light diet.

DIARRHOEA. Isolate the dog in case there is any infection. Give milk to drink instead of water, and do not feed solid food. Arrowroot or cornflour pudding is better. Sometimes one of the well known makes of diarrhoea powder is helpful. Keep the dog warm and call your Veterinary Surgeon if the condition persists after twenty-four hours.

EARS. Canker is a possible trouble especially with the spaniel type drop ears, and so it is essential to keep the ears clean. Should you find canker, first clean out the ear carefully with spirit on cotton wool and ask your veterinary surgeon to advise you as to the best ear drops to use.

EYES. Colds are shown by watering of the eyes and if taken in hand at once can be quickly cured. I find it handy to keep a tube of THIAZAMIDE EYE OINTMENT for these. You can get one from your Veterinary Surgeon. If you want to bathe the eye use boracic and water or plain (kitchen, not table) salt and water, either of these are better than any patent eyewash! For eye injury or bad ulceration you will need professional advice.

FRACTURES. Immobilise the limb and consult a Veterinary Surgeon.

HERNIA. Puppies quite often get an umbilical (or

navel) hernia at birth, usually caused by the dam pulling on the cord when she is separating the puppy. As long as the hernia is soft and remains small (about the size of a pea) it can be ignored as it will not cause any trouble even if it occurs in a bitch required for breeding.

INGUINAL HERNIAS are almost always on the left side and only seen in bitches. Again, as long as they remain small they cause no trouble and can be left alone. If they increase in size then it is better to have them operated on, especially if the bitch is to breed. It is not a dangerous operation.

Occasionally one gets small dog puppies showing hernias in the groin. These are sometimes visible and sometimes disappear and re-appear again looking quite big in proportion to the small puppy. Although rather worrying at first these are best forgotten, as in most cases, by the time the puppy is about four months old it will have disappeared altogether. If, by the time the puppy is over about four months, the hernia is still visible consult your Veterinary Surgeon.

HIGH TEMPERATURE AND FEVER. Keep dog warm and quiet. Isolate, and consult your Veterinary Surgeon.

NORMAL TEMPERATURE. A dog's normal temperature is $101\frac{1}{2}°$. On a hot day, or after vigorous exercise, or excitement, the temperature may rise higher temporarily. This need not cause anxiety as long as it does not reach a high temperature. e.g. 103° or more.

SKIN TROUBLE. Unless it is a simple eczema or scurfiness that you are sure you recognise, it is wisest to consult a Veterinary Surgeon. For eczema there are various suitable ointments on the market. Scurfiness can be cured with 'Vaseline' hair tonic as a rule, or a 'Vosene' shampoo.

WORMS. The coat is apt to be 'Starey' and the dog may drag its behind along the floor; usually it eats voraciously but seems to keep very thin. Puppies particularly get thin but their tummies get very distended and 'blown out'. For adult dogs give one of the well-known worm remedies as directed on the packet. There are several very good capsule type worm remedies on the market which, incidentally, do not require the dog to be starved before dosing. Small puppies should be dosed at six weeks old when they are weaned, whether or not worms are known to be present. For this BANOCIDE is very good and does not seem to upset even tiny puppies. The dose is $\frac{1}{4}$ tablet for each 2 lb. body weight and no starvation is required. You must get a prescription from your Veterinary Surgeon for this, or he may supply the pills to you. I use it again at three months, just before teething, for all my puppies. It is not a good thing to worm puppies while they are teething (from three – six months) but it is quite a good idea to give them a further dose just after they are six months.

There are many other illnesses, accidents, etc. that can happen to a dog. You will find one of the numerous small paper books published by Canine firms such as Bob Martins, Sherley's, Spratts, Benbows, and others, give a lot of useful information on many of these things. If you think something is wrong with your dog that you cannot recognise or understand, do go to your Veterinary Surgeon for advice, and go in the early stages.

CHAPTER VII

The Brood Bitch

THE BROOD BITCH should be the best you can afford for she needs to be well-bred and of good type, as well as being sound and healthy and with no really bad faults. In fact if you stick to what I have said with regard to buying a bitch in a previous chapter on 'choosing dogs for show' you will not go far wrong with your brood bitch.

As a rule a bitch puppy will have her first heat any time between about six months and one year, or even later in some cases. A puppy born from December to April is more likely to 'come in' young than say a puppy born from May to November. This is because during cold weather bitches seem less likely to come into season than when the weather is warmer. On the whole I think perhaps the second season is probably the best time to breed from a bitch for the first time but, if the bitch does not have her first season until she is eleven months or over, then I think it perfectly reasonable to breed from her then, provided she is strong, healthy, and well-developed.

Before the bitch is due in season you should study her pedigree and make up your mind as to the choice of a suitable stud dog. Don't just rush in and mate her to the dog that happens to be winning most at the moment, on that score alone. He may be, in fact almost certainly is, an extremely nice dog – obviously he must have 'what it takes' in the show ring. But will he suit your bitch? Is his type right for her? And above all what about his pedigree? – that is most important. Lastly, even his colour must be considered. Then, supposing the pedigree is very satisfactory in view of your bitch's breeding, what about any puppies he may have sired. Have you seen them, and do they measure up to his type and standard? It does seem to me that there is one side of choosing a mate for a bitch that is often over-looked. Plenty of people seem all too willing to rush off and get their bitch mated to the big winner of the moment, but it seems that comparatively few people do what, to me, would seem an even obvious thing to do – that is to consider the desirability of using the sire of this wonder dog that is winning all before him. After all the sire has surely proved beyond doubt that he *can* produce 'the goods' to a bitch of the type and breeding that suits him. What is this winning son's dam like? Would my bitch be likely to suit the sire as well? Having answered these questions you then have to consider whether or not you feel it worth trying. These are the sort of deliberations which make breeding interesting, and such deliberations are necessary for breeding to type.

Having decided on the stud dog of your choice make a provisional booking for the bitch with the owner of the dog, at the same time indicating as far as you can when she is due in season. As soon as she actually starts her season get in touch with the stud dog owner to confirm that the dog will be free, and arrange about the mating. The best time for this will more often than not be between the tenth – fifteenth day after the bitch has started to come on heat, and the most likely time will be twelfth, thirteenth or fourteenth day, although there are exceptions. I have had two different bitches, sent to stud dogs of mine, that would mate on the ninth day and no other, but I think this is pretty rare. Normally I like to have a maiden bitch on the tenth day, if she comes from a distance, so that I can keep her and see that she is mated on the most suitable days. I usually let the dog serve the bitch twice if it is convenient to do this.

The stud fee is paid for the service the dog renders in mating the bitch, therefore it is customary for this fee to be paid to the owner of the dog *at the time of mating*. Some people have the idea that the fee is paid for the puppies that will be born and therefore do not want to pay until the bitch has whelped, but this is wrong. All stud fees should be paid when the bitch is mated and the cost of returning the bitch to her owner after the mating should be added if the stud dog owner has to arrange to do this. There may of course be other arrangements made between the owner of the dog and the owner of the bitch such as choice of puppy or puppies in lieu of stud fee, in which case individual arrangements are agreed upon at the time and should be written out in duplicate and signed by both parties, each keeping a signed copy. This will avoid difficulty and muddle when the litter arrives.

The bitch returns home after the mating and must of course be carefully confined until she is no longer attractive to male dogs. Apart from care over this, there is no need for any special treatment or feeding for the next four – five weeks. About that time it should begin to be apparent that she is in whelp, or not, as the case may be. If an owner wants to know earlier than this, most veterinary surgeons can tell by examining the bitch between the twenty-first and twenty-eighth day, I believe. In any case there is no need to embark on extra feeding until the fourth – fifth week. If you are sure then of the success of the mating you can increase the food, giving plenty of milk if the bitch will drink it (some bitches will not take milk before the puppies are born), plenty of meat, some raw, but not too large a proportion of biscuit at this time, cut that out a bit in favour of more meat. During the last month before the birth is due it is a good idea to give 'Stress' once a day, either in milk with a little glucose added or mixed up with the food. This is a calcium and mineral compound which can be bought quite inexpensively at Boots and many other chemists and dog shops. It is in my experience very valuable both for the bitch and later for her puppies. I also give all my bitches two tablespoonsful of raspberry leaf tea over their food or in their milk once a day before whelping. This may sound like a real old wives' tale, but I have proved to my own satisfaction that it is a most useful and effective way of ensuring a clean birth with no trouble over retained after-births and their attendant bother and worry. It is very simple to make. You buy dried raspberry leaf from Boots or one of the Herbal shops. This will probably last you for two or possibly three bitches as the leaf, being dried can be kept safely for a long time. All you do is to put about a dessertspoonful into a jug and infuse it by pouring about $\frac{1}{2}$ pt. of boiling water over it, just as you do with tea leaves. This quantity can be kept for several days, giving the bitch some each day, and making another infusion when that is finished. I give this up to, and for a couple of days after, the birth. Apart from this the bitch lives normally, with plenty of fresh air and moderate exercise, until it becomes obvious that the puppies' arrival is imminent.

CHAPTER VIII

Whelping

THE LITTER is due to be born sixty-three days after the mating. I have the bitch sleeping in my bedroom for the last week of her pregnancy. For this I have a child's playpen with a floor, and ½ in. wire netting fixed all round the bars. I put a dog box in one corner lined with newspaper and an old blanket and the bitch sleeps there. Should she start to whelp I can hear her and be up and around to put her in a whelping box in the place where the puppies are to be born. This of course is a warm room. The whelping box will be lined with scruffed up newspaper and I shall have plenty of thick newspaper on the floor all around the box. I shall also have beside me a smaller box or basket with blankets in and around an alumininium hot water bottle inside a thick wollen bag. This is because, as soon as a puppy is born, it is put to the mother while she cleans it but, when another puppy is imminent, I always take any already born and put them in the separate box with the hot water bottle just while 'mum' is busy with the newest arrival. In between births she has the puppies again as the sucking helps the next one to be born.

THINGS YOU NEED FOR THE WHELPING

Basin, warm water, soap, Dettol or other similar disinfectant for washing your hands.

Towel.

Some *clean rags* for cleaning and drying puppies.

A pail into which you can put afterbirths, dirty rags, paper etc.

Plenty of spare newspaper.

Pair of blunt ended sharp surgical scissors.

Pair of Spencer Wells forceps.

Milk or water and glucose for the bitch to drink if she is thirsty during the whelping.

THE WHELPING BOX. This should be large enough for the bitch to lie in fully stretched out, and the sides should not be too high to make it easy to attend to the bitch and puppies. It is a very good idea to have rounded bars put all round the insides of the box about $2\frac{1}{2}$–3 in. above the floor of the box and about 1–$1\frac{1}{2}$ in. away from the sides. These bars can be kept away from the sides by screwing them in with the screws going through empty cotton reels put between the bars and the sides of the box. A box made like this will keep the bitch from lying right against the sides, so that should a puppy get between her and the side it isn't so likely to get squashed or suffocated.

Normally, if all goes well, the bitch starts scratching up bed, blanket, paper – anything handy – in a rather desperate and furious manner, usually biting at it as well. This makes a noise and will wake you if you are asleep or dozing and, as a rule, you will have time to put her where you want her to whelp, get your hot water bottle filled and paper on the floor, before the first puppy arrives. At first you will notice the contractions at intervals, not very strong and not very frequent, then as the moment gets nearer the contractions become stronger and the intervals between them shorter until with a big heave you will suddenly see the rather jelly-like looking bag emerge. When you see this get down by the box and try and note that it is the head of the puppy you can see inside the bag. If the bitch does not at once start licking and tearing the bag open you can get it open and, with a clean little finger, get the puppy's mouth open and clean it out, this will enable it to start breathing the air. However, if the bitch is managing all this quite expeditiously leave her to do it and don't interfere. If, when you look at the bag, you *don't* see the head of the puppy do not on any account try and burst the bag. If the puppy is coming feet first let it be completely born in the bag before you try to burst it. It is quite possible, and in fact very often happens, for a puppy to be born quite easily in spite of the fact that it does not come head first. The only danger is that if the bag gets burst and the head is not born very quickly then the puppy may drown in the liquid. So never try and burst the bag if the head is not born. Your best hope is for the bag to remain intact until the whole is born then, and only then, get it open at the head end and open and clear the mouth as quickly as you can if the mother is not attending to it. At the same time holding the puppy in the palm of one hand in such a way that there is no pull on the cord.

The time to call the vet comes if the bitch has been having frequent contractions at close intervals for a long time and no puppy arrives. Once the contractions are really strong and coming very frequently the puppy should arrive in a matter of a few minutes. With most bitches puppies are born at anything from ten or fifteen minute to half-hour intervals roughly. One might be a bit longer and there are exceptions when this happens, but it is more usual for them to be born at not longer than an hour between puppies. If you feel the bitch has been having contractions for a long period with nothing happening, it is wise at least to telephone your vet for advice. He will then tell you what to do and come if he feels it is necessary.

During the whelping, if all goes well and the bitch is managing adequately by herself, do not interfere. But there are times when help is needed. For instance it is as well to see that, when the puppy is born and the bitch busy cleaning it, the cord is not pulling on the puppy's tummy – this is often the cause of a navel hernia – but can be stopped if you can hold the puppy in the palm of your hand keeping the cord slack until the afterbirth has come away or the mother has bitten the cord off. If the afterbirth is not born you may find it necessary in certain circumstances to tie cotton tightly round the cord about an inch from the puppy's tummy, then clip a pair of Spencer Wells forceps on the cord on the far side of the cotton from the puppy, leaving enough room between forceps and cotton to cut the cord with a pair of scissors. This will free the puppy, and the forceps will prevent the afterbirth from slipping back and it will probably be born quite soon or with the next puppy.

Some bitches, particularly young maidens, will bite off the cord very close to the puppy so that bleeding is profuse. It is then necessary to act very quickly and tie the cord very tightly close up to the tummy with cotton, in order to stop the puppy bleeding to death. It is a tricky thing to do when bleeding is taking place, but can be managed and is the safest thing to do. It is not very safe to try putting on Spencer Wells forceps if the cord is bitten off very close to the tummy.

However, this sort of thing is not really for a novice coping with a first litter unless she has nurse's or other medical training. You cannot learn these things from a book, only by practical experience. If possible, do try and watch someone experienced handle some whelpings before you tackle one on your own. Failing that try and get someone, who is experienced, to sit with you and be ready to help and advise you in coping with your first litter.

In any case it is always advisable to warn your Vet that you are expecting a litter and make sure you have one who will come during the night if necessary. Even an experienced person never knows when more skilled veterinary help maybe needed. What he or she does know is the right moment to call in that extra skilled help.

After whelping, having made sure there are no more puppies, put the bitch out for a minute to make herself comfortable. Clear up all the dirty paper and mess, putting clean dry blankets in the whelping box, tuck the bottle with its cover on under the blanket in the corner in cold weather (you won't need it if it is summer or warm). Then let 'mum' settle down with her babies all snuggled up to her, give her some warm milk and glucose if she wants it and let her settle down for a well earned rest.

Eclampsia

This is a condition sometimes met with in bitches after whelping, while nursing the litter. It is due to a calcium deficiency, the bitch being unable to store sufficient calcium in the body to supply her own and the puppies' needs. It usually occurs five or six weeks after the birth, but may do so even as early as three weeks after. The bitch becomes very restless, jumping in and out of her box, and her eyes look bloodshot. She is apt to pant a lot and there may be paralysis of the legs. It is important to contact your vet immediately you recognise these symptoms because early treatment in the form of a Calcium and Vitamin D injection will quickly restore the bitch to normal. If this injection is not given the attack may prove fatal. It is generally advisable to take the puppies off the bitch and hand feed after such an attack. I have found that 'Stress' given every day during the pregnancy and while nursing helps to prevent Eclampsia.

CHAPTER IX

Rearing the Puppies

DURING the period after the puppies are born the bitch must have enough suitable food for herself and the puppies – plenty of milk, meat, eggs, and of course fresh water always available. I also give the nursing mother glucose in at least one of the milk drinks each day, and also continue with the 'Stress' she has been having once a day for the past month. 'Farex' or 'Farlene' is also useful as an addition to the milk.

The puppies exist for the first three weeks of life on the bitch's milk. When three weeks old they can begin weaning, starting with some fresh scraped raw beef. This should be scraped off with a sharp knife, always working along the grain of the meat, not across it. Each puppy starts with a little ball of scraped meat about the size of a moderately large pea once a day, increasing the amount slightly each day from three weeks old. The way to feed the scraped meat is to open the puppy's mouth and, with the finger, put a small amount on the roof of the mouth near the front. The puppy will be able to eat this easily and will soon get to like it enough to take it from your hand and then from a saucer. It is important not to start by putting the meat on the tongue, or at the back of the mouth, for this is not easy for the puppy to cope with and may make him choke. At four weeks I add warm milk and glucose to the diet, and at five weeks they have five meals a day – three of milk and glucose or

mixture of half milk and half water with a little glucose or honey. This must of course be fed warm but not too hot. The puppy will need about half a teaspoonful of this mixture at each feed. After a week you can increase the amount gradually to about a teaspoonful at each feed and you can let them miss out the 2.00 a.m. and 4.00 a.m. feeds, which will give you a little extra time for sleep. At two weeks old you can claim your night's rest and feed only three hourly during the day increasing the size of the feeds still. When the puppy is three weeks old you can start feeding scraped raw meat just as you would if the puppy were being reared naturally by the dam, continuing with the milk feeds and increasing the gaps between feeding times gradually, and from then go on as you would with a normal litter. Some people like to add a very small quantity of Virol to one of the milk feeds each day. I would give 'Stress' in one milk feed a day after the second week.

When the puppy is still very small it must be made to perform its natural duties. This is done after meals by gently massaging the tummy and by just stroking the penis or vulva, as the case may be, with a soft small paint brush or a piece of cotton wool. See that the puppy is clean and dry before you put it back on it's warm blanket. A little talcum powder is a good thing to dry the skin and keep it nice, but don't use *too much*.

You will have to be sure a hand-reared puppy is really strong before attempting docking or dew claws and it will probably be better to do them a little later than the usual time.

CHAPTER X

The Stud Dog

I WOULD not recommend a novice or beginner to embark on a dog at public stud until he or she has had quite a bit of experience. The management of a stud dog and the successful mating of bitches is not the sort of thing to learn from reading a book. It really is necessary to have practical instruction. The owner of the stud dog has to take a great deal of responsibility in accepting a valuable bitch for mating, and therefore must be thoroughly competent to see that the mating is successfully achieved, and that no harm is done to the dog or the bitch as a result of careless handling of the matter.

It is neither fair nor right to accept a bitch to mate, shut her up in a room with the dog for a time, and later hand her back to the owner and take the stud fee. The dog may or may not have earned it, but you certainly have not!

If you are keen to keep a stud dog, your best plan would be to employ an experienced handler to take charge of the matings and teach you at the same time.

To be of any real value a stud dog must have a good pedigree and, preferably, should do well in the show ring; this will have given breeders a chance to see him and judge whether he is the type they want to use for their bitches. After his first few litters, if he is found to be siring good stock, he will have plenty of calls on his services.

The dog you choose for a stud should be of a strong masculine type, with no glaring faults, and plenty of good points to recommend him. He should be sound, have a good temperament, and most certainly should not be a nervous dog. The ideal dog is one who knows his job, gets on with it without fuss or bother, and is not easily put off by a difficult or snappy bitch. If you have such a dog you are lucky. It is really better to wait until you can breed a dog good enough for stud yourself. If you feel you must buy from someone else, it might be a good idea to go to a breeder who has very good stock, but who does not care to keep stud dogs. You would possibly get a very good dog from such a person, whereas, if you buy from a breeder who keeps stud dogs, he will obviously want to keep the best for himself.

The stud needs good feeding, with a generous allowance of meat in his diet, proper exercise, and he must of course be kept scrupulously clean. With a young dog it is a good thing to let him have his first bitch when he is ten or eleven months old, and the bitch should be an experienced brood, rather than a maiden, if possible. You may have a little trouble teaching the dog, not what he is expected to do, (he probably knows that!) but just how you expect him to set about it. On the other hand he may be the type that knows it all by instinct and will get on with it very satisfactorily on his own. It is always better to train your stud dogs from the start to allow you to hold the bitches for them. This is really a safeguard; a bitch may try to pull away from the dog or struggle and this can cause injury to either or both of them. If you are holding the bitch you can ensure this does not happen. I train my own cavaliers to mate on a rubber covered grooming table or bench rather than on the floor, as I find it a great deal easier to handle a small breed at that sort of height. It is certainly very much more comfortable and less tiring than getting oneself into an awkward and uncomfortable position on the floor, especially with a long mating. So far I have never found any difficulty in training my dogs to do this, but I know some dogs do not like being off the floor.

I prefer not to feed a stud dog within an hour or so of the time he is to mate, and this also applies to the bitch. They will both need an opportunity to exercise immediately before mating. When they do meet, let them have a little time to make each other's acquaintance and do a bit of courting before the actual mating. When this takes place most dogs, at some point, will 'turn and tie'. For those who do not know, the dog starts the act of mating with his front paws and the front half of his body up over the bitch's back, and they are both facing in the same direction. When he turns for the tie, he will get both his front legs to the ground to one side of the bitch, bringing the one back leg which is on the opposite side over her back, so that all four feet are on the ground. The dog will then stand back to back against the bitch. He may remain like this for two or three minutes or for a longer period, maybe 20, 30, or as much as 45 mins. It is during this tie it is very important to see that the bitch does not pull away from him, and thus risk a rupture for either of them. The way to be sure this does not occur is by getting both dogs' tails close together, holding them in one hand as near the roots of the tails as you can, with the ends of the tails sticking up above the backs of the dogs. This will ensure that they cannot pull away from each other.

When the dog has completed the act he will gently come away from the bitch. Many people pick her up and hold her on their laps on her back for a few minutes before putting her down again, but I am not sure that there is really any benefit to be gained from doing this. It is a good idea to put her somewhere where she can rest quietly for a while. Do not put her with other bitches to rush around, and do not put her out to exercise immediately after mating. Having put the bitch back, check that the dog is tidy and normal and put him out for a few minutes. If you have other stud dogs do not put the one that has just had a bitch back with them for a little while in case the smell of the bitch makes them jealous and causes a scrap.

It is not a good thing to overwork your stud dog at any time during his career. There are other things to be considered as well as cashing in on every stud fee you can lay your hands on. It is better to have a reasonable number of bitches at fair and suitable intervals and keep your dog on top of his form, siring good strong stock, than to have a few too many stud fees in a short period and find that bitches are missing to him or siring poor litters of inferior puppies. With a young dog, after his first bitch I like to leave him about three months before he has another, and keep to fairly good intervals for the next few bitches. If you offer a dog at public stud it is your duty to do all in your power to ensure that the matings result in good strong healthy litters, and it is certainly in your own interest to do this. When I accept a bitch for mating I like to have the opportunity of allowing the dog to serve her on two days. It is also my practice to allow any bitch that fails to produce a litter as a result of the mating to be served again by the dog at her next season without further fee, provided the owner lets me know within a week of the time the puppies should have arrived. I feel this is a fair and reasonable thing to do. This should not be expected however, for some people argue that the stud fee is not for the litter, but for the services of the dog, and if there is no resulting litter that is just too bad, and it may be the fault of the bitch as much as of the dog.

13. CHAMPION MILLSTONE BEECHKING TANSY. Black and Tan bitch. *Sire:* Millstone Eustace. *Dam:* Highstead Renee. Born 17.6.70. Owned by Mrs. E. M. Booth. Bred by Mr. and Mrs. R. Clarke.

14. CHAMPION KERSHOPE SANDON PARK ICEBREAKER.
Blenheim Dog. Born 19.1.72. Owned by Miss C. L. M. Gatherall. *Sire:* Ch.
Pargeter McBounce. *Dam:* Sandon Park Crystal. Bred by Park.

15. CHERRYCOURT WAKE ROBIN

It is therefore as well to ask the owner of the dog you intend to use, at the time you are arranging the stud, whether he or she does allow a second, free service in the event of the bitch missing. There is no rule about it.

It is not essential for the dog to turn and tie, or for the mating to be a long one, to result in a satisfactory litter. I have known good litters to be produced after the shortest of matings with no turn and tie.

CHAPTER XI

Shows and Showing

IF YOU WANT to go in for regular showing you must only compete at shows which are authorised by the Kennel Club, otherwise you will be banned from showing at the 'official' dog shows. There are several different types of shows held with the official permission of the Kennel Club, and you will find these advertised in the weekly dog journals published on Fridays (*Dog World* and *Our Dogs*) and they both supply the necessary information about shows etc.

Starting with the biggest and most important type of show we have *The Championship Shows*. General Championship shows which cater for all breeds of dog. Cruft's Show is of course the biggest and best known of these, and is held early in February each year. In such a show you get classes for all sorts of different breeds judged by people 'passed' by the Kennel Club as being qualified in the particular breed which they judge. Usually there are also variety classes in which dogs of different breeds may compete against each other. Some of the General Championship shows take two, or even three days, with the different groups of dogs being judged on different days. These groups are Gun dogs, Hounds, Terriers, Non-Sporting, and Toys, plus the Obedience dogs. If you are interested in one particular breed and want to visit the show to exhibit or to see this breed you must make sure from advertisements, or from a schedule, which of the days your breed will be on show.

The second type of Championship Show is what is known as a specialist show and this will only cater for one breed, or for the different varieties of one breed as in the case of *Poodles* and other breeds which are divided into different sizes and types of coat, each type having a separate Breed Register.

Both these types of Championship Show are so called because at these shows, and these only, two challenge certificates are awarded by the Kennel Club for each of the breeds. These are given, one for the best dog and one for the best bitch exhibited in the particular breed if, in the judge's opinion these dogs are good enough to be given the title of champion of their breed. In order to gain the right to *use* the title 'Champion' before their names each dog must have been awarded three such challenge certificates, under three different judges. There is a special rule about this for gun dogs, which of course does not concern this breed.

The next largest type of show is the *Open* Show. Again these may cater for numerous different breeds and variety classes or may be for only one breed. In fact they are very similar to the Championship shows except for the fact that entry fees and prize monies are lower than at the championship shows, and no challenge certificates are offered for competition, also the judges do not have to be 'passed' by the Kennel Club before being appointed. Their choice is left to the discretion of the Show Committee.

Next we have *Limited Shows* either for a variety of breeds or just one breed. Competition at these is confined to members of the particular society holding the show. Judges chosen by Committee, as at Open Shows. *Sanction Shows* are small shows, confined to members of the Society holding the show. A 'variety' sanction show may have twenty classes only, and a one breed sanction show may have only ten classes. Judges chosen by Committee as at Open and Limited Shows.

At any of the above shows obedience classes may also be held. *These shows are all held subject to Kennel Club rules* which means, among other things, that every dog shown must be registered at the Kennel Club and that entries must be made by the date specified as the closing date for entries. The closing date may be anything from about a month to a fortnight *before* the date on which the show is held. No late entries may be accepted and no dog that has not been entered for the show may be taken inside the show ground or hall. So, if you have your pet dog with you, but not entered for the show, you may not take him in but must leave him outside while you go in yourself.

There are also many very small shows held, all over the country, and often in connection with Flower Shows, Fêtes, Church Bazaars etc. These are called *Exemption Dog Shows* and are described as being held 'with Kennel Club Permission' but they are exempt from Kennel Club rules and so dogs need not be registered to be exhibited at them. Showing at these shows does *not* debar you from showing the dog at any of the other shows I have already mentioned. The promoters of these Exemption Shows have paid a small fee to the Kennel for permission to hold them and are allowed four classes for pedigree dogs, but these classes must be for a variety of breeds and are not allowed to be for only one breed. They may have for instance classes for Any Variety Puppy, or Any Variety Gun Dog, or Any Variety Sporting dog, or Any Variety Terrier, or Toy dog, and such like, but may not have a class for Poodles only, or for Cavaliers only etc. They are also allowed to hold Novelty classes, as well as the four pedigree classes. A novelty class being something like 'Dog with longest tail' or 'best eyes', or 'best mongrel dog', and such like. You can usually enter for these shows beforehand or actually on the show ground, and usually the entry fees are quite small with a slightly reduced entry fee if you enter before the day of the show. They are generally advertised locally in shops etc. and in the local papers.

How to enter for a show

Before you can show your dog at an 'Official' show he must be registered with the Kennel Club. To do this you must obtain a form from the Kennel Club, fill it in according to the instructions and send it back to the club with the fee. If the show entry form has to be posted before you get your registration certificate back, you enter the dog under your first choice name (on registration form) adding the letters (N.A.F.) after it, signifying that you have applied for the name.

Write to the Secretary of the show and ask for a schedule to be sent to you. This will give you all the information you need to know and will have an entry form with it which you must fill in and sign and send back completed, with the entry fee money, to the Secretary not later than the closing date for entries. In due course you will receive an Exhibitor's pass, which will admit you to the show with your dog. If, when you get to the show you do not know quite what to do ask for help from another exhibitor. You will generally find someone willing to give a helping hand to a novice.

Having arrived at the show and had your dog 'vetted' at the door, if it is a 'benched' show you must find what number your dog's bench is, either from your Exhibitor's pass, or, if it isn't on that, from a catalogue, which can be purchased in the show. Cavaliers, being Toy dogs, are normally 'Benched' in wire pens mounted on long trestle tables. You should have with you a blanket to put down on the floor of the pen for your dog to lie on. It is advisable also to have with you a small bottle of disinfectant and a rag so that you may disinfect the pen before you put your blanket and dog into it. If the show is 'Unbenched' you will have to find yourself a seat where you can sit with your dog and your belongings until it is time for you to go into the ring to be judged.

OTHER THINGS YOU NEED TO TAKE TO THE SHOW:

A good brush and comb.

A light collar and lead or a slip lead, which the dog must wear in the show ring.

A feeding dish and the dog's food.

A small bottle of drinking water (You can usually, but not always, find a tap at the show, so it is better to have some with you).

A few tit-bits if you think this will help your dog to show better.

It is also useful to have some means of cleaning the dog if you have had to walk him to the show and it is wet. To clean a dog with white legs and feet dry with a leather or towel, then sprinkle the fur with some cheap bay rum (Boots have small sprinkler bottles of this) and then shake on some light powdered magnesia (Boots also sell this in packets). A small flour tin with a sprinkler top or an old talcum tin makes a good sprinkler for this. Leave it for a minute and then brush all the powder out using the brush the way the coat lies only. You will find the coat is nice and clean and this is a better method than using a chalk block. Only use the powder on the white part of the coat.

You may feel a bit strange at your first show but you will soon get used to the show atmosphere and after one or two you will know just what to do and what 'luggage' you need to take with you. Some people seem to arrive with everything but the kitchen stove!

Preparing a dog for show

Blenheim dogs should be bathed the day before a show with a good shampoo or mild soap and water. Some people put beer in the rinsing water and some use fine oatmeal in the rinse, both to make the coat soft and silky. A little blue is also used for rinsing by some people but can easily spoil the look of the coat if a little too much is used.

Tricolours are really better washed several days before the show in order that the shine can be got back into the black parts of their coats, while the whole colours are really better not washed near a show. They should be really well-groomed and 'polished' with a velvet so that their coats have a nice sheen.

After bathing the dog must be thoroughly well rinsed to be sure all the soap is out of the coat, then well dried. It is not a good thing to rub the coat the wrong way with a rough towel; a nice big leather, used in the direction the coat lies all the time, is much better and gives a good silky finish to the coat. Some people put an old nylon stocking on the dog and use a hair dryer, or dry with the dryer combing the coat in the direction of the lie all the time. The main thing is to get the dog dry leaving the coat flat and silky and not curly or rough looking. When it is dry, good brushing and polishing with a velvet is needed.

Never take your dog into the show ring in a dirty condition. Not only does it spoil his chances and look nasty, but it is most unpleasant for a judge to have to handle dirty dogs. If a dog is worth showing he is certainly worth the trouble of seeing he looks his best when he goes into the judging ring.

Records

When you are showing it is important to keep details of the wins of all your dogs in a record book. This will enable you to see quickly the classes any one dog is eligible to be entered for, and will prevent you entering them in a class for which they are not eligible and having them disqualified, and losing your prize money and being fined by the Kennel Club. It is also a good idea to record the judges' names against the wins. This will help you to know which judges seem to like your type of dog for future showing.

CHAPTER XII

On Breeding

Colour in breeding

THE dominant colour is Blenheim.

Blenheim × *Blenheim* will produce Blenheims. If Blenheims are mated to Blenheims for several generations the pigment may tend to deteriorate and light eyes and pink or brown noses may be found in the puppies.

Blenheim × *Tricolour* will produce Blenheims and Tricolours together or litters containing only Blenheims or only Tricolours.

Blenheim × *Ruby* will produce Rubies and Blenheims but these latter will only occur if the ruby parent carries particolour blood. You may get mismarked rubies from this mating, i.e. Rubies with white on them.

Blenheim × *Black and Tan* may produce any of the four colours if the Black and Tan parent carries particolour blood. It is not a very good mating as mismarked whole colours are likely to occur, also very heavily marked particolours. Pigment of eyes and nose is usually good from this mating.

Tricolour × *Tricolour* will produce Blenheims and Tricolours.

Tricolour × *Black and Tan* may produce all four colours provided the Black and Tan parent carries particolour blood. You may get heavily marked tricolours. Rubies are usually a good rich colour with black nose pigment and dark eyes. Nose and eye pigment in the Blenheims and tricolours usually very good.

Tricolour × Ruby. The same as Tricolour × Black and Tan, particolours only occurring if the Ruby parent carries particolour blood.

Ruby × Ruby produces Rubies and Blenheims, the latter only when both parents carry particolour blood.

Ruby × Black and Tan a good mating for getting whole colours. It may also produce both particolours if both parents carry particolour blood.

Black and Tan × Black and Tan may produce all four colours but the particolours only occur if both parents carry particolour blood.

Line Breeding and In-Breeding

These are two different things and many novices cannot understand the difference between them.

Line breeding means breeding to a line and type rather than out-crossing all the time to outside lines. It is a good way to establish type but naturally must only be carried out with good, strong, healthy stock to be successful, and you must know your pedigrees well to carry it out.

The simple formula for line breeding is that 'the Sire of the Sire should be Grandsire of the Dam on the Dam's side'. If you want to line breed you look at your bitch's pedigree. It goes like this.

		Grandparents
	Parents	
	London King	London Squire
		London Maid
Royal Princess (your bitch)		
	Royal Maid	Regency Buck
		Queen of the May

Regency Buck is your bitch's grandsire on the Dam's side, so when you want to mate your bitch you look for a good typical son of Regency Buck to mate her to.

In-breeding is very different and is used far more on the continent than it is here. It is not very popular in England. This consists of mating daughter to father, mother to son, brother to sister, or half brother to half sister, or son or daughter to their own grandparent. It is true that these sort of matings do sometimes produce brilliant results, that is why some breeders do in-breed. It is also true that done with weak or faulty stock it can produce disastrous results such as bad faults, cleft palates, hare-lips, eye troubles, and many other abnormalities and undesirable faults. It is certainly not a practice that is wise for a novice to indulge in.

PEDIGREES. It is very helpful in breeding to study pedigrees and learn how the best dogs are bred. You can learn a great deal from them.

How to set about being a Breeder

If you are going in for breeding and showing do learn all you can, and I can assure you there is a tremendous lot to learn about dogs and dog-breeding. It is only those people who have been doing it for from three – five years who know it all! After that you begin to realise all the time how much more you have to learn. It is an extremely interesting hobby to take up and offers endless scope. It also offers very good companionship, both human and canine.

Read, mark, learn, and inwardly digest everything, from the weekly dog papers to the things you can learn by watching the shows and hearing the people around you talk. Sort it and sift it and glean all you can, it will all help your enjoyment and later on you may want to try your hand at judging. Don't rush in too soon. This is a difficult and responsible task. The novice has a lot to learn to make him competent to carry it out, and it cannot be learnt in a year or two, even if you have been lucky and had your share of winners. It is a very good training to go and learn to steward not only your own breed but any other that opportunity offers. That in itself is not the easy job some people think it is, but you can learn a tremendous lot from it by watching the top class judges at work and by watching the dogs in the ring. It is a useful and interesting job and well worth while for the knowledge you gain about Kennel Club rules, which you obviously have to learn and know, about shows and procedure, and the way to set about judging. You can also learn to be a better exhibitor.

Then do enjoy your breeding and showing. It is not a matter of life and death. It is a game, and can be such an enjoyable one if you are ready to make it so.

Appendix

BREED CLUBS

Cavalier King Charles Spaniel Club
Secretary: Mrs. D. Archer, Jia Kennels, Rockland St. Mary, Norwich NOR O8W.

Scottish Cavalier King Charles Spaniel Club
Secretary: Mrs. M. Smith, Riddle Mill, Lilliesleaf, Melrose, Scotland.

West of England Cavalier King Charles Spaniel Club
Secretary: Mrs. D. Fry, Priestlands, Gloucester Road, Hambrook, Nr. Bristol, Avon.

Northern Cavalier King Charles Spaniel Club
Secretary: Mrs. E. Nelson, 1 Rutland Road, West Bridgeford, Nottingham.

Cavalier King Charles Spaniel Club of Ireland
Secretary: Miss C. R. Macartney, Harbour Grace, 4, Grey Point, Helens Bay, County Down.

Three Counties Pekingese and Cavalier Society
Secretary: Mrs. B. M. Blackmore, Jasmin Cottage, Horton, Wem, Salop.

KENNEL CLUB

1 Clarges Street, Piccadilly, London, W1Y 8AB
Publishers of *Kennel Gazette* (monthly).

WEEKLY DOG JOURNALS

"Dog World" Idle, Bradford, Yorks.
"Our Dogs", 1 Oxford Road Station Approach, Manchester.

Index